# SPORTS GREAT OSCAR DE LA HOYA

# —Sports Great Books—

## BASEBALL

**Sports Great Jim Abbott**
*0-89490-395-0/ Savage*

**Sports Great Bobby Bonilla**
*0-89490-417-5/ Knapp*

**Sports Great Orel Hershiser**
*0-89490-389-6/ Knapp*

**Sports Great Bo Jackson**
*0-89490-281-4/ Knapp*

**Sports Great Greg Maddux**
*0-89490-873-1/ Thornley*

**Sports Great Kirby Puckett**
*0-89490-392-6/ Aaseng*

**Sports Great Cal Ripken, Jr.**
*0-89490-387-X/ Macnow*

**Sports Great Nolan Ryan**
*0-89490-394-2/ Lace*

**Sports Great Darryl Strawberry**
*0-89490-291-1/ Torres & Sullivan*

## BASKETBALL

**Sports Great Charles Barkley**
**Revised Edition**
*0-7660-1004-X/ Macnow*

**Sports Great Larry Bird**
*0-89490-368-3/ Kavanagh*

**Sports Great Muggsy Bogues**
*0-89490-876-6/ Rekela*

**Sports Great Patrick Ewing**
*0-89490-369-1/ Kavanagh*

**Sports Great Anfernee Hardaway**
*0-89490-758-1/ Rekela*

**Sports Great Juwan Howard**
*0-7660-1065-1/ Savage*

**Sports Great Magic Johnson**
**Revised and Expanded**
*0-89490-348-9/ Haskins*

**Sports Great Michael Jordan**
**Revised Edition**
*0-89490-978-9/ Aaseng*

**Sports Great Jason Kidd**
*0-7660-1001-5/ Torres*

**Sports Great Karl Malone**
*0-89490-599-6/ Savage*

**Sports Great Reggie Miller**
*0-89490-874-X/ Thornley*

**Sports Great Alonzo Mourning**
*0-89490-875-8/ Fortunato*

**Sports Great Hakeem Olajuwon**
*0-89490-372-1/ Knapp*

**Sports Great Shaquille O'Neal**
**Revised Edition**
*0-7660-1003-1/ Sullivan*

**Sports Great Scottie Pippen**
*0-89490-755-7/ Bjarkman*

**Sports Great Mitch Richmond**
*0-7660-1070-8/ Grody*

**Sports Great David Robinson**
**Revised Edition**
*0-7660-1077-5/ Aaseng*

**Sports Great Dennis Rodman**
*0-89490-759-X/ Thornley*

**Sports Great John Stockton**
*0-89490-598-8/ Aaseng*

**Sports Great Isiah Thomas**
*0-89490-374-8/ Knapp*

**Sports Great Chris Webber**
*0-7660-1069-4/ Macnow*

**Sports Great Dominique Wilkins**
*0-89490-754-9/ Bjarkman*

## FOOTBALL

**Sports Great Troy Aikman**
*0-89490-593-7/ Macnow*

**Sports Great Jerome Bettis**
*0-89490-872-3/ Majewski*

**Sports Great John Elway**
*0-89490-282-2/ Fox*

**Sports Great Brett Favre**
*0-7660-1000-7/ Savage*

**Sports Great Jim Kelly**
*0-89490-670-4/ Harrington*

**Sports Great Joe Montana**
*0-89490-371-3/ Kavanagh*

**Sports Great Jerry Rice**
*0-89490-419-1/ Dickey*

**Sports Great Barry Sanders**
**Revised Edition**
*0-7660-1067-8/ Knapp*

**Sports Great Deion Sanders**
*0-7660-1068-6/ Macnow*

**Sports Great Emmitt Smith**
*0-7660-1002-3/ Grabowski*

**Sports Great Herschel Walker**
*0-89490-207-5/ Benagh*

## OTHER

**Sports Great Michael Chang**
*0-7660-1223-9/ Ditchfield*

**Sports Great Oscar De La Hoya**
*0-7660-1066-X/ Torres*

**Sports Great Steffi Graf**
*0-89490-597-X/ Knapp*

**Sports Great Wayne Gretzky**
*0-89490-757-3/ Rappoport*

**Sports Great Mario Lemieux**
*0-89490-596-1/ Knapp*

**Sports Great Eric Lindros**
*0-89490-871-5/ Rappoport*

**Sports Great Pete Sampras**
*0-89490-756-5/ Sherrow*

# SPORTS GREAT
# OSCAR
# DE LA HOYA

John Albert Torres

—*Sports Great Books*—

**Enslow Publishers, Inc.**

44 Fadem Road          PO Box 38
Box 699                Aldershot
Springfield, NJ 07081  Hants GU12 6BP
USA                    UK

BIO
DE LA
HOYA

**Library of Congress Cataloging-in-Publication Data**

Torres, John Albert.
    Sports great Oscar De La Hoya / John Albert Torres.
        p.  cm. — (Sports great books)
    Includes index.
    Summary: Discusses the personal life and boxing career of the fighter who won an
Olympic gold medal in 1992 and went on to become a professional champion.
    ISBN 0-7660-1066-X
    De la Hoya, Oscar, 1973– —Juvenile literature. 2. Boxers (Sports)—United
States—Biography—Juvenile literature. 3. Boxers (Sports) [1. De la Hoya, Oscar,
1973– 2. Mexican Americans—Biography.] I. Title. II. Series.
GV1132.D37T67 1999
796.83'092—dc21
    [B]                                      98-1202
                                                CIP
                                                AC

Printed in the United States of America

10 9 8 7 6 5 4 3 2 1

**Illustration Credits:** AP/Wide World Photos.

**Cover Illustration:** AP/Wide World Photos.

26277

# Contents

# *Chapter 1*

The crowd was in a frenzy. Finally the moment everyone was waiting for had arrived. Ring announcer Michael Buffer made it official with his famous battle cry: "Let's get ready to rumble!"

The Golden Boy, Oscar De La Hoya, was set to box one of his boyhood idols, Julio Cesar Chavez, for the World Boxing Council (WBC) Super Lightweight Championship (140 pounds). The fight was taking place at Caesar's Palace in Las Vegas, Nevada, on June 7, 1996. De La Hoya carried a 21–0 record into the ring and had already won three world titles. Many boxing experts felt that the twenty-three-year-old De La Hoya had the potential to become one of boxing's greatest fighters. Facing Chavez was his first real test. Chavez, known as one of the all-time great fighters, had once knocked down De La Hoya during a sparring session, when De La Hoya was just seventeen years old.

When boxers practice fighting each other, they are sparring. They usually wear protective equipment, such as headgear and a mouthpiece so that no one gets hurt. Usually a well-known fighter will spar against young, up-and-coming boxers, to get ready for a fight. That sparring match, however, had taken place a long time ago.

Knocking down a young Oscar De La Hoya may have given Chavez a false sense of security. "I don't need to watch training tapes [of Oscar]," Chavez boldly declared. "He's tasted my power and he's not going to want to taste it again."

De La Hoya, on the other hand, had great respect for his opponent, the thirty-four-year-old Chavez, who had a record of 97–1–1. "He [Chavez] has all the experience in the world, [almost] 100 fights," De La Hoya said before the fight. "That's going to be to his advantage. He's very dangerous because he hits so hard."

De La Hoya studied videotapes and styles of many famous boxers to get ready for the fight. He watched tapes of boxing greats Sugar Ray Robinson, Willie Pep, and Sandy Sadler.

He especially admired Pep's style. "Now there was a fighter," he said about Pep. "He'd go 15 rounds and never get hit. He was a technician, more like a matador. Boxing to me is an art form," he continued. "It's not just trying to knock someone out. I try to hit and not get hit. I love boxing but I hate fighting."

The national anthems of both Mexico and the United States were sung, and the fighters seemed eager to begin. De La Hoya looked up at the Las Vegas sky during the anthems and thought of his dead mother; he winked up at the sky.

At the opening bell, De La Hoya, weighing 139 pounds and wearing multicolored shorts, went right after Chavez. He felt it was important to dictate the pace of the fight. De La Hoya did not want to get into a slugfest with the 139-pound Chavez, who was known for his powerful right-hand punches. De La Hoya kept Chavez away with his long stiff left jab. He jabbed Chavez above the right eye twice in a row. Then, at the

2:08 mark of the first round, De La Hoya nailed Chavez with a straight right hand in the same spot. Chavez was cut badly. De La Hoya's three consecutive punches had opened a very deep cut. Chavez began to bleed heavily.

De La Hoya's punches often cut other fighters. He twists his gloves at the moment of impact, creating a bruising effect, trying to cut his opponent's face.

Like any good fighter, De La Hoya could tell that Chavez could not see very well with blood in his face. De La Hoya blasted Chavez with several more right hands to the face, scoring as many points as he could. De La Hoya stalked Chavez patiently around the ring, as Chavez bobbed and weaved, trying to avoid further damage.

Between the first and second rounds, Chavez had his cut looked at and patched up by his cornerpeople. Every fighter has a few people in his corner. These people, also known as seconds, include his trainer, a cut man, and sometimes the fighter's manager.

In round two, Chavez came out very aggressively. He sensed how badly he was cut, and he knew that he could not last long. Chavez, with the heart of a champion, knew he would have to hit De La Hoya with a few bombs to take him down. But De La Hoya was ready. His long jab kept Chavez away; then he would counterattack. His strategy was to keep Chavez backing up. A fighter cannot fight if he is constantly backing up. Backing up too often causes a fighter to tire quickly. After two rounds, De La Hoya had thrown 101 punches, and a frustrated Chavez had thrown only 49.

By the fourth round, De La Hoya was clearly in control of the fight. Chavez was still bleeding badly and seemed unable to get through De La Hoya's defense. The large Hispanic-American crowd that had been rooting for the Mexican legend,

In 1996, Oscar De La Hoya (left) had to fight his idol, Julio Cesar Chavez, for the WBC Super Lightweight Championship.

Chavez, could sense that the end was near. They urged Chavez to fight harder.

Chavez came out strong to start the fourth round, and he stung De La Hoya with a strong pair of straight lefts. De La Hoya was shaken for a moment, but he quickly used his long arms to keep Chavez at bay. Soon De La Hoya had Chavez backing up, and the crowd was on its feet. Everyone sensed that this could be the last round of the fight.

With one minute left in the fourth, De La Hoya pummeled Chavez with a left hand, followed by a strong left hook. He set himself and delivered a hard right to Chavez, followed by a brilliant combination, a series of different punches grouped together to form a dangerous attack. De La Hoya capped off his flurry with a smashing right-handed uppercut that broke Chavez's nose. Now blood poured from Chavez's right eye and from his nose. The ringside doctor stopped the fight, with twenty-five seconds left in the round. De La Hoya was awarded a technical knockout (TKO). A technical knockout is awarded when a doctor or referee (or both) decides that the opposing boxer is too hurt, or cut too badly, to continue fighting. A TKO can also be awarded if a fighter is knocked down more than three times in any one round. With this TKO, De La Hoya had won his fourth championship belt and his twenty-second fight without a defeat.

De La Hoya jumped up and down in celebration. He leaped up onto the ropes and waved to the fans. The Golden Boy had defeated a legend. It was a dominating performance. No one could have predicted that De La Hoya would have destroyed Chavez with such relative ease. The fight, which was scheduled to go twelve rounds, lasted only four. Oscar De La Hoya was no longer a rising star; he was now a superstar.

"Unfortunately, I did go up against my idol," De La Hoya told television reporters after the fight. "It was a tough fight for

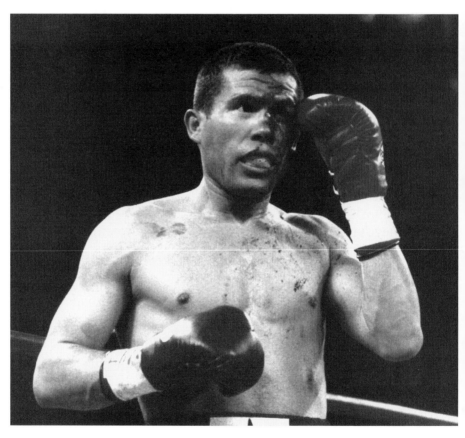

The referee had to stop the fight in the fourth round. Chavez was bleeding heavily from the constant flurry of De La Hoya's punches.

me. I dedicate it to my mother and to all the fans who supported me throughout the world."

When asked what the future would hold, De La Hoya joked with reporters. "I'm going to the movies," he told them.

Oscar De La Hoya had accomplished so much in so little time. At the age of twenty-three, he had already won an Olympic gold medal, twenty-two professional fights, and four championship belts. These titles were the World Boxing Organization (WBO) Junior Lightweight, the WBO Lightweight, the International Boxing Federation (IBF) Lightweight, and now the WBC Super Lightweight.

De La Hoya showed no signs of slowing down, even after moving up a weight class. He already held titles in the 130-pound class and the 135-pound class.

Another goal that De La Hoya hoped to achieve was to win over the Mexican fans. De La Hoya is a Mexican American, but they have never really accepted him. Sometimes De La Hoya gets hate mail and nasty letters from Hispanic-American boxing fans who want him to lose.

"Hate mail from my own people hurts," De La Hoya said. "Maybe it's jealousy. But I want to break that barrier."

Maybe it is just that De La Hoya keeps beating every Mexican fighter who faces him in the ring. "Unfortunately, Oscar has had to fight very popular Mexican guys," said boxing promoter Bob Arum. "But they will have to love him. They won't have anybody else."

# *Chapter 2*

Oscar De La Hoya was born on February 4, 1973, to Cecelia and Joel De La Hoya, in Los Angeles, California. Oscar grew up in a poor neighborhood called a barrio, in East Los Angeles.

Oscar grew up within an extended family. His grandfather, Vincent, and his grandmother, Candelaria, also lived with Oscar and his family. Oscar also has a brother, Joel, who is a year older than he, and a sister, Ceci, who was born when Oscar was nine years old.

It was on Christmas Day in 1976 that Oscar De La Hoya's life was changed forever. There were three pairs of boxing gloves under the Christmas tree that year—one pair for Oscar, one pair for his older brother, Joel, and one for Oscar's dad, Joel, Sr.

From that moment on, Oscar loved to box. He would box with his brother, but most of the time he would box his dad, who went on his knees to box with his sons. Oscar wanted to wear the gloves all the time. It was the best Christmas present he ever received.

15

It was not a surprise that Oscar would like boxing at such a young age. Boxing was, after all, in his blood. Oscar's grand-father, Vincent, was an amateur boxer who fought in Mexico in the 1940s in the featherweight division. Oscar's dad, Joel, Sr., was a good professional fighter in his own right, with a record of 9–3–1 as a lightweight in the United States. Joel, Sr., born in Mexico, was sixteen years old when he immigrated to the United States. He was very poor, and he hoped that boxing would be his road out of poverty.

Joel De La Hoya quit boxing when he realized that he was not good enough to become a champion. To support his family, he got a warehouse job for an air-conditioning company.

"My father and my grandfather both had been boxers, so

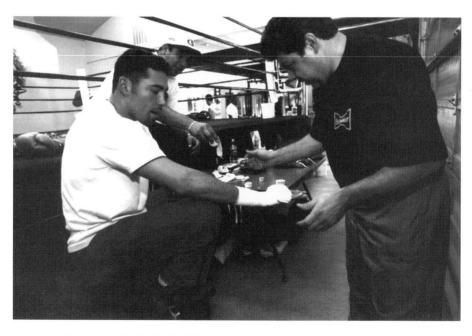

Boxing runs in the De La Hoya family. De La Hoya's father and brother had both tried their hand at boxing. His brother, Joel, (rear), is helping the trainer prepare Oscar De La Hoya for a fight.

there was a lot of talk about that around the house," Oscar De La Hoya said.

Oscar was five years old when his father first took him to a boxing gym. He immediately enjoyed it. "I loved it," he said. "The first day I put on the gloves, being up there, running around the ring, it was fun for me."

Oscar would ask his father to take him to the gym every single day—even Sundays! He trained for a full year at the Pico Rivera Boys' Club before he was allowed to have his first fight. Oscar fought his first fight when he was six years old. He beat up his opponent, another six-year-old. The boy ran from the ring crying.

"I hit him and he started crying, and started bleeding," De La Hoya recalled. "I didn't feel bad for him. Inside, I felt good, very good. It was natural for me."

Oscar was already a powerful puncher. He won a trophy that was bigger than he was. Many of the old men who watched the fight gave Oscar dollar bills as his "reward."

Boxing was not the only challenge that Oscar and his family faced. Just a few city blocks away from where they lived, there was an area known for its gangs, criminals, and drugs. Oscar's parents were determined to keep their children away from those mean streets. They taught their children good values and stressed education. Oscar's mother, Cecelia, became very involved in her children's studies and stressed to them that good grades were the only sure way out of the barrio. De La Hoya says that his mother was the main influence on his life.

Many of Oscar's friends were in gangs. They asked him to join many times. He always refused. "I knew that if I worked hard and got a good education, I would have a future," he said.

Besides boxing, Oscar also loved to draw. He was a talented artist. Many of his sketches and paintings hung on the walls of his home. Art was his favorite subject in school. As a

17

kid, Oscar also loved to ride his skateboard. He enjoyed his mother's cooking as well. His favorite food to this day is tacos.

By the time Oscar was ten years old, he began training at the Resurrection Boys' Club in East Los Angeles. The run-down building had once been a church. Now it represented the only way out of the barrio for many Mexican-American children. In the barrio most of the boys dreamed of being boxers. Oscar was one of those rare kids who understood the type of commitment that is needed to make a dream come true. When he was not in the gym, he was running mile after mile through his neighborhood streets or jumping rope in front of his home. Running and skipping rope are two ways that boxers build up their endurance. This type of work is called roadwork.

The kids in Oscar's neighborhood respected him from a young age because of his great fighting skill. Oscar did not look very tough, though. He was very skinny, graceful, and shy.

Oscar had the full support of his entire family. He said that was a major key to his success. "They are always there for me," he said. "If I needed a new pair of gloves because they [the old pair] were too old or worn out, my uncle would give me money to buy some. All my uncles would get together and buy me stuff because they saw my potential and believed that I could be something in boxing."

Oscar began studying under Manuel Torres, director of boxing at Resurrection. Oscar's father, Joel, still taught him, as well. Soon Oscar had a hard time finding sparring partners for his workouts. He had been urged by Torres and Joel not to take it easy during sparring. They did not want him to get lazy or to develop any bad habits in the ring. They also wanted him to develop a killer instinct. This is the ability to put a fighter down even when you know that he is hurt, tired, or in trouble.

Oscar bloodied a lot of noses during sparring, and many of the other kids shied away from him.

Oscar officially began his amateur boxing career while he was in junior high school. It continued through his time at Garfield High School, in Los Angeles. It was at Garfield High that Oscar really developed a keen interest in architecture. He took all the art and drafting courses that he could.

By the age of fifteen, Oscar was entering many tournaments and was winning them easily. Oscar won the national Junior Olympic championship in the 125-pound weight class. This was an impressive win because Oscar faced the best fourteen- and fifteen-year-old fighters in the country. His boxing career was going smoothly, but sometimes it got in the way of

Growing up in Los Angeles, Oscar De La Hoya attended Garfield High School. These Garfield High School students went to the NBC studios to support De La Hoya as he went on *The Tonight Show*.

his schooling. He was forced to miss a lot of classes during his senior year, due to boxing tournaments. He had private tutors travel with him, and he was able to get a lot of the schoolwork in advance so that he would not fall behind.

His boxing commitments also put a serious strain on Oscar's social life. He understood, and he made these sacrifices without question. Some things, however, still stick in his mind.

"I was fighting the night my high school prom was going on," he said. "It was a dual meet against a Cuban team at Fort Bragg. After I beat the Cuban, I called my girlfriend, my high school sweetheart. She went to the prom with her brother. I missed it," he continued. "I told myself that I would make my own prom."

At the age of sixteen, Oscar was considered a senior amateur boxer. This meant that he was now eligible to enter the Golden Gloves tournament. Held every year, the Golden Gloves is the most famous amateur boxing event in the United States. In the Golden Gloves tournament, a series of local and regional bouts lead to the final championship matches.

As in every other tournament Oscar had entered, he cut through the competition with ease. He swept through local, regional, and finally national competition to become the featherweight (126 pounds) amateur champion of the United States. Boxing is divided into weight classes. This is done so that only boxers of similar weight can fight each other. A fighter can move up in weight class to fight a heavier opponent if he wishes, but this is usually only done in the professional ranks.

Oscar's next goal would be to represent the United States at the next Olympics. He started training with the help of Roberto Alcazar, a former boxer who worked with Oscar's father, Joel, at the air-conditioning company.

"Oscar is so different from the boxers that I have worked

with," Alcazar said, "because he knew what he wanted to do with his life at an early age. He realized he wanted to be a boxer."

In the summer of 1990, Oscar was named as part of the twenty-four-member United States boxing team that would participate in the Goodwill Games. The team flew to Seattle, Washington, to fight in what was considered a good Olympic tune-up.

During this time, Oscar's family experienced tragedy as well as triumph. Oscar's mother, Cecelia, became seriously ill with cancer. Oscar's parents did not want to distract or worry

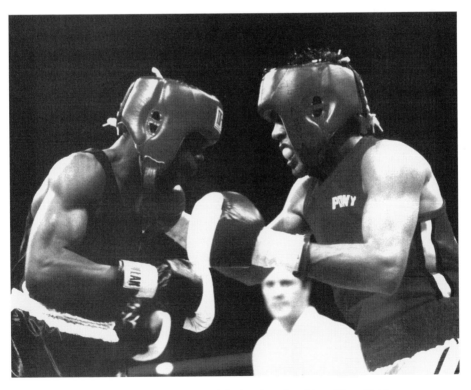

De La Hoya (right) delivers a right hand to the chin of Ivan Robinson during the 1990 Goodwill Games.

Oscar during the tournament, so they did not tell him. His mother even refused treatments on days that Oscar was scheduled to fight. It was more important to her to be able to cheer him on. Oscar called her his best friend.

As usual, Oscar was great throughout the tournament. He used his crafty style and his powerhouse right hand to defeat Lee Sang-Hun of South Korea, Airat Khamatour of the Soviet Union, and Ivan Robinson of the United States to win the championship. Oscar was now the world's greatest featherweight amateur.

Oscar's celebration was very short. When the family returned home to East Los Angeles, Oscar's father sat him down and told him how sick his mother was.

Cecelia died two months later, at the age of thirty-nine. Before she died, she told Oscar that her dream was for him to win an Olympic gold medal. He promised her that he would win one in her memory. It was a promise that Oscar simply could not break.

# Chapter 3

Oscar knew that winning an Olympic gold medal is one of the hardest things for an athlete to achieve. Thousands of fighters from all over the world train and compete for one medal.

At his mother's funeral, a weeping Oscar vowed to devote every ounce of his energy to granting his mother's final wish.

Oscar trained harder than ever. He was obsessed with his desire to win. Oscar woke every morning before dawn to do his running. He usually ended up running to the cemetery where his mother was buried. He wanted to be near her. Seeing his mother's burial site inspired him to work even harder. When he was supposed to rest, between rounds of sparring, Oscar would shadowbox or jump rope. Shadowboxing is boxing against your shadow, or against an imaginary opponent.

Oscar's next big challenge was the 1991 United States Olympic festival to be held in Los Angeles. He was very confident going into the tournament. He had not lost a match in more than five years, and he would not lose here. He breezed through the tournament and then defeated Patrice Brooks to capture the lightweight (132 pounds) championship. It was

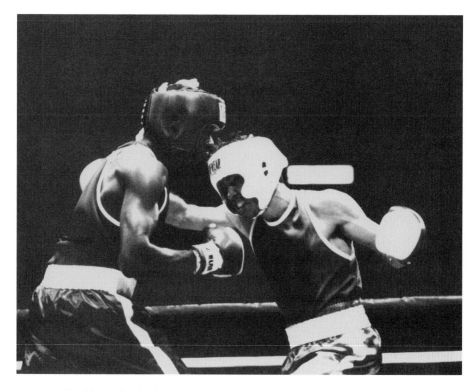

Looking to land a knockout punch, Oscar De La Hoya (right) tries to hit Patrice Brooks with a left hook.

here that Oscar began a new tradition. After winning the fight, he always knelt down on one knee in his corner and blew a kiss to his mother in heaven.

"This is for you, Mom," he would say.

Shortly after the festival, Oscar De La Hoya graduated from Garfield High School. He had a big decision to make, but it was an easy one. His plans to go to college and become an architect would have to wait. De La Hoya was a well-known amateur boxer now. A promising and profitable boxing career was clearly in his future. A boxing career would not wait until he graduated college. The time was now.

Besides, De La Hoya had made a vow to win the gold medal in the 1992 Summer Olympics. Although he did not lack self-confidence, he still received a lot of encouragement from people who believed he would be a successful boxer.

"The kid has all the tools. Right now, based on what I've seen, he has the gold medal," said Pat Nappi, who coached the United States Olympic boxing team from 1976 to 1984.

De La Hoya did not want to let his art skills fade, however. He kept them sharp by drawing and sketching. He often sketched his family, friends, coaches, and other boxers. He was proud of the fact that he was multitalented.

At this time, De La Hoya was enjoying his newfound celebrity status. People in the neighborhood treated him like a star. One time, he got mugged as he was walking home. When the two robbers realized that they had mugged Oscar De La Hoya, they went to his house and returned the wallet and all the money inside it. They did not want to rob the local hero. Oscar De La Hoya was truly a celebrity.

In November, De La Hoya and the rest of the United States boxing team flew to Sydney, Australia, to compete in the World Amateur Championships. In amateur competition, bouts are scored on a points system, with boxers receiving points for landing clean punches. This differs from professional fights, in which boxers earn points for winning a round.

What took place in Sydney would have a great impact on De La Hoya's future as a boxer. He won all of the preliminary fights with the usual ease. Then, in the championship fight, De La Hoya squared off against the tough Marco Rudolph, the German champion.

Rudolph beat De La Hoya to the inside punch and punished him with some bruising body shots. Rudolph kept very close to De La Hoya, not allowing him to get any punching room. With De La Hoya's long arms in check, Rudolph won the decision, 17–13.

Although De La Hoya was very dedicated and well trained, he may have become a little overconfident. He had not lost in so long that he felt unbeatable. "It was the best thing that ever happened to me," he said of the loss. He realized that his hard work was not enough. He would have to give it everything he had. He would have to reach deep inside and work even harder if he wanted to keep his promise to his mother.

Though he had been a member of the United States team at the World Amateur Championships, De La Hoya now had to fight in the Olympic trials in order to make the 1992 Olympic team. With the Olympic trials only a few months away, De La Hoya began putting in even more time at the gym. He sparred more rounds than ever and increased his running from five miles a day to six. De La Hoya and Alcazar then really began working on De La Hoya's left jab. It is very important to have a good jab, since that punch can serve many purposes. First of all, a jab can be used defensively to keep opponents away. It can also be used offensively to tire and sting the other boxer or to set up combinations or other punches.

The hard work paid off. De La Hoya swept through the Olympic trials and was named to the 1992 United States Olympic boxing team. In July, the team flew to Barcelona, Spain, for the start of the games. De La Hoya felt very comfortable in Spain. He is fluent in both Spanish and English, so he was able to communicate with athletes from all over the world. Oscar De La Hoya was one step closer to fulfilling his promise.

"It's like an obsession to get that gold medal," he said. "That's the main reason I want to go to the Olympics, to fulfill the promise I made to my mother."

Alcazar and Joel De La Hoya, Sr., accompanied him to Barcelona. Then De La Hoya's entire family received money from important people in boxing, who wanted to represent his professional career. The money was used to send the family to Barcelona to cheer him on.

While De La Hoya was one of the best boxers on the American team, not many people thought he would win his first Olympic bout. De La Hoya, fighting in the 132-pound (lightweight) class, went up against tough Adilson Silva, of Brazil.

De La Hoya was cut by Silva early in the fight and had to be inspected twice. A disqualification due to an injury would have meant the end of De La Hoya's dream, but he rallied in time to knock out Silva late in the third round.

De La Hoya also won fights against Moses Odion of Nigeria and Tontcho Tontcheu of Bulgaria, but he was the underdog for his next match. This time he was set to fight the South Korean champion, Song Sik Hong. De La Hoya did not feel very strong. The long tournament was wearing him down. Hong ran across the ring and attacked him at the opening bell. Hong turned the fight into a brawl that resembled a wrestling match. He kept using his shoulders and elbows to keep De La Hoya away. One time he even put De La Hoya into a headlock.

De La Hoya fought back, but late in the second round he had three important points deducted from his score. Still, he held on to defeat the crafty Korean champion by the score of 11–10.

"We were just lucky," Olympic boxing coach Joe Byrd said. "It could have gone either way."

There was only one fight left now. Only one fighter stood in the way of winning the gold medal and fulfilling his promise to his mother. He was Marco Rudolph, the only fighter who had ever beaten De La Hoya during international competition. De La Hoya was looking forward to avenging his 1991 loss to Rudolph. Things would be difficult, though, for

De La Hoya had suffered a very bad thumb injury to his right hand during the fight against Hong.

De La Hoya rested and soaked his hurt right hand as he studied tapes of his earlier loss to Rudolph. Before the final fight, Joel De La Hoya offered his son some advice: "You're taller than he is," he said, "and you've got a longer reach. You've got to take advantage of these things."

De La Hoya came out of his corner very aggressive, as he sensed how close he was to achieving his dream. He out-punched and outhustled his German opponent. De La Hoya was basically able to use his right hand only for blocking Rudolph's left hooks. It hurt too much to punch with.

In the second round, De La Hoya hurt Rudolph with a solid left hook to the jaw as the round was ending. Rudolph was clearly stunned, and he stumbled back to his corner. The third round was dominated by De La Hoya. Rudolph was now very leery of his left hook, so De La Hoya began using his hurt right hand to land big body shots. With one minute left in the fight, De La Hoya knocked Rudolph down with a tremendous left hook. Rudolph dragged himself up off the canvas and took a standing eight count. (The referee must count to eight every time a boxer stands up, after he is knocked down and gets up before the count of ten.) De La Hoya poured it on, never giving Rudolph a chance. He won the bout, 7–2. He had kept his promise to his mother. Oscar De La Hoya had won a gold medal.

After the fight, De La Hoya said that he wasn't really nervous during the match, even though he knew he could use only one of his hands. "I felt my mother right next to me during the whole fight," he said. "I knew she was there taking care of me."

De La Hoya dropped to his knees after the fight and blew a kiss toward the sky for his mother. Then he ran around the ring

De La Hoya won the gold medal in the Lightweight Division at the 1992
Summer Olympics. The games were held in Barcelona, Spain.

with an American flag in one hand and a Mexican flag in the other. "The American flag was for my country, and the Mexican flag was for my heritage," he later explained.

When De La Hoya received his gold medal, he stood out on the medal podium and saw his family crying for joy. "I saw my father and the rest of my family crying. I didn't cry because my mom would have said 'Don't cry, you won the gold medal, be happy.'"

Oscar De La Hoya was the only American fighter to win a gold medal at the 1992 Summer Olympics in Barcelona. Upon returning home to the United States, he had a stop to make before going home. He went to the cemetery and draped his gold medal around his mother's tombstone.

De La Hoya's amateur boxing career could go no farther. Although it was his mother's hope that he would not become a professional fighter, he realized the amount of money that was waiting for him. He had the chance to earn millions of dollars and become a champion. He wanted to take care of his family. He wanted to repay everyone who had helped him along the way.

A whole new chapter was beginning in Oscar De La Hoya's fighting career.

# *Chapter 4*

Boxing managers engaged in a virtual bidding war for the right to represent De La Hoya's professional career. They saw a handsome, educated young man, a gold medal winner, and a fighter who would appeal to Hispanic Americans and other fight fans. Basically, they saw a Golden Boy, which now was De La Hoya's nickname.

Many fight experts predicted that De La Hoya would be the next Sugar Ray Leonard. But De La Hoya wanted to be the first Oscar De La Hoya.

Oscar realized, however, that there is a big difference between amateur and professional fighting. Amateur fights last only three rounds, and fighters are equipped with headgear to prevent injury. Professional fights last ten to twelve rounds, and there is no protective headgear. There is always a big risk of injury during a professional fight.

The managing team of Shelly Finkel and Lou Duva had done De La Hoya and his family a lot of favors. They had already invested a lot of money in his future. Finkel and Duva had followed his career since 1990. They were hoping that they had the inside track to managing his pro career, but De La Hoya and his family received an offer that they just could not refuse.

The management team of Steve Nelson and Robert Mittleman pursued De La Hoya strongly. They knew that De La Hoya was someone special who could make a lot of money for everyone associated with him. "Oscar was good-looking and bilingual and he hit as hard as anyone," Nelson said. "We felt that he'd be a marketable commodity."

In the fall of 1992, De La Hoya signed a contract with Nelson and Mittleman. The deal included roughly $500,000, a couple of cars, and a $565,000 house in the exclusive Montebello section of Los Angeles, where De La Hoya's mother had always dreamed of living. The deal also allowed him to keep Alcazar as his trainer.

Meanwhile, Finkel and Duva felt cheated. They thought that they had a strong oral agreement with De La Hoya. Finkel later sued De La Hoya and recovered most of his $100,000 investment.

De La Hoya was not bothered by this management controversy. He let his father handle most of the contract negotiations. De La Hoya just wanted to start fighting and start winning. He had amassed an incredible amateur record of 223–5, with 153 knockouts. The knockout total is extremely impressive. Mittleman and Nelson chose Bob Arum to promote De La Hoya's fights. He was ready for his first professional fight.

Oscar De La Hoya started his pro career on November 23, 1992. He picked up exactly where he had left off as an amateur, knocking out Lamar Williams in the first round with a devastating left hook. He was quickly 1–0.

De La Hoya's left hook left a strong impression on

De La Hoya looked impressive during his first fight against Lamar Williams. De La Hoya knocked out Williams in the first round.

Mittleman. "I've never seen anything like it in my life," he exclaimed. "What a left hand!"

De La Hoya then knocked out Clifford "Bobo" Hicks, also in the first round, for his second victory. Next, it took him only two rounds to knock out Paris Alexander, to run his record to 3–0.

Mittleman was choosing De La Hoya's opponents very carefully. He wanted to pick fighters who were good, yet beatable. It was important to give him a lot of confidence and to show fight fans that he would be a good professional fighter. "I was letting him fight guys who were tougher than Arum thought they were," Mittleman said. "But Oscar was a thing of beauty."

In February of 1993, De La Hoya scored a technical knockout in the fourth round against Curtis Strong. Then, he knocked out Jeff Mayweather in four rounds as well. De La Hoya was 5–0, with 5 knockouts.

De La Hoya was unable to register a knockout in his sixth fight, against a tougher opponent named Mike Grable. Grable came into the fight sporting a 13–1–2 record, but De La Hoya knocked him down in the second round. Grable got up and danced and pranced and ran from him the rest of the fight. Remarkably, Grable lasted all eight rounds of the fight, despite being knocked down seven times. De La Hoya won an easy decision.

De La Hoya won his next four fights by knockout, including one over Troy Dorsey. Dorsey had been a former featherweight champion. Next, his eleventh fight would turn out to be a little different, and it would lead to drastic changes.

In October of 1993, De La Hoya fought a little-known Mexican lightweight by the name of Narcisco Valenzuela. Early in the first round, De La Hoya was knocked down by Valenzuela. De La Hoya was furious. He jumped back up on his feet and knocked out Valenzuela thirty seconds later. Oscar was now 11–0 but was unhappy with his progress. He and his father felt he needed a new trainer, someone with more experience. "Alcazar [De La Hoya's trainer] wasn't doing a bad job," Mittleman recalled. "But the father got nervous. He wanted a new trainer."

That November, De La Hoya's team hired former lightweight champ Carlos Ortiz to become his trainer. Alcazar, who had trained De La Hoya since he was a kid, was very unhappy.

Oscar De La Hoya (left) connects with a shot to the face of Angelo Nunez. De La Hoya defeated Nunez to improve his record to 10–0.

De La Hoya blamed Nelson and Mittleman for Alcazar's unhappiness and fired them that December.

Oscar De La Hoya decided to manage his own career, with his father's help. He kept both trainers, which proved to be a mistake. Ortiz and Alcazar never got along, and it caused problems for De La Hoya in his next few fights.

In his second fight with the new trainers, a relatively unknown fighter by the name of Giorgio Campanella knocked De La Hoya down in the first round. De La Hoya eventually recovered, and he knocked out Campanella in the third round. A few fights later, he was wobbled, and he almost went down against a soft puncher named Johnny Avila in the seventh round. He won that fight as well, but questions about his durability were arising.

Many boxing experts wondered if De La Hoya was soft, or if he had a "glass chin." A fighter who gets knocked down easily, or does not take a punch to the chin too well, is said to have a glass chin.

De La Hoya felt that it was just a case of being too eager. He was impatient in his quest to knock out opponents. His defense was bad, and he was walking into punches that he should have been blocking. "I've explained to all the people involved in boxing," he said, "that it's not that I have a weak chin. Or that if I get hit, I'll go down. Anybody will go down. [Mike] Tyson, [Sugar Ray] Leonard, [Muhammad] Ali, they all went down. Nobody has a chin. If somebody gets hit right, they're going down."

Even after a few average outings, Bob Arum still felt that Oscar De La Hoya could be something very special. "Oscar can become one of the greatest fighters of his generation," he said. "There's only one thing that can stop him, like it stopped a lot of other guys. If he loses focus."

De La Hoya makes sure that focus is never a problem. He

Oscar De La Hoya knows the importance of training. He is a tireless worker who wants to enter every fight in top shape.

lives and breathes boxing. Even his private life is filled with boxing reminders. His two dogs are boxers, of course. He named them Sandy and Willie, after the great fighters Sandy Sadler and Willie Pep.

Besides playing with his dogs and playing golf, De La Hoya also loves driving fast cars and going fishing. In fact, his favorite place to be, when he is not boxing, is Cabo San Lucas, Mexico. Cabo is known for its great sport fishing.

De La Hoya and Arum secured De La Hoya's future even further when they signed a whopping five-year, $21 million contract with cable giant Home Box Office (HBO) to televise De La Hoya's fights. An exclusive deal like that is very rare and sometimes risky with a young fighter who has only fought eleven times.

HBO president Seth Abraham was not worried. "Oscar could be the biggest attraction we've ever had, even if he loses a few," he said.

De La Hoya was also beginning to get exposure doing endorsements and commercials. He signed deals with B.U.M. Equipment Clothing, Champion Athletic Wear, and Edge Shaving Gel.

Endorsement agent Franklin K. Wheaton compared De La Hoya to Michael Jordan because of both Jordan and De La Hoya's ability to appeal to a broad range of people.

With all those other pieces in place, De La Hoya was about to fight for his first championship. He was set to fight Denmark's Jimmi Bredhal for the WBO Junior Lightweight title on March 5, 1994, in De La Hoya's hometown of Los Angeles.

The fight was held in the city's newly renovated Olympic Auditorium and was geared toward Los Angeles's large Hispanic-American population. It was proclaimed Oscar Night, and fans chanted "Oscar! Oscar!" from the opening bell. However, many seats were empty, because De La Hoya was still not fully accepted by the Hispanic-American fans.

Bredhal was undefeated in sixteen fights, and it was his first fight outside Europe. It was De La Hoya's first fight since he had fired his managers nearly five months before.

De La Hoya came out very aggressive, and it looked as if it would be his night. He knocked down Bredhal in the first and second rounds, with hard right hands to the head. Bredhal recovered enough to last ten rounds before going down again in the tenth.

Bredhal's right eye had become swollen and puffy. Dr. Bob Karns stopped the fight and awarded De La Hoya a TKO victory and his first championship. Bredhal rushed over and hugged Oscar, who was now 12–0.

It was the first time De La Hoya had gone beyond eight rounds, and he looked and felt great. It was also the first time he fought at the 130-pound weight class. He had always been around 135 pounds.

"I felt very strong," De La Hoya said. "I felt I was in command. I felt strong and powerful and fast."

Oscar De La Hoya was now a professional champion. His goal was to win titles in five more weight classes. He would have to win many more fights and overcome a lot more obstacles.

# *Chapter 5*

De La Hoya did not wait long to defend his new championship belt. On May 8, 1994, he knocked out Italy's Giorgio Campanella in the third round, despite being knocked down himself in the first round. On August 8, he stepped up in weight class to fight former champ Jorge Paez for the vacant WBO Lightweight Championship. After being knocked out in the second round by De La Hoya, Paez was left dazed and impressed. "I've never been hit that hard by a punch before," Paez said after the fight.

In February 1995, De La Hoya fought former two-time International Boxing Federation (IBF) Junior Lightweight Champion John John Molina. De La Hoya was 16–0 entering the fight, and Molina was 36–3. De La Hoya scored a first-round knockdown and scored a lot of points with his jab. Then Molina changed his style. He started rushing De La Hoya like a bull. Molina would hold on and punch inside, scoring points and bullying De La Hoya all over the ring.

Even though he was winning, De La Hoya was still walking into and taking punches that he should have been blocking.

He was getting knocked down far too many times. It seemed as if he would probably soon be knocked out by a lesser fighter. Alcazar, De La Hoya's longtime trainer and cornerman, had no answers or instructions. Alcazar did not know what to do against such a fighter. The fight lasted all twelve rounds, and De La Hoya won a tough and very close decision.

A shaken De La Hoya tried to show confidence after the fight, even though he was very concerned about the lack of instruction from his corner.

"John John Molina had three punches: a right, a left, and his head," De La Hoya joked. "It was an easy fight, I just wasn't ready for his head."

De La Hoya felt that he was not improving the way that he should be, so he told Bob Arum that he needed a new trainer. This time, Alcazar had no objections. De La Hoya fired Ortiz, demoted Alcazar, and hired a legendary Mexican trainer, Jose Rivero. Arum had recommended the retired trainer, who was known in boxing as the Professor.

Despite all the problems, Oscar De La Hoya had improved his record to 17–0. Rivero's first task was to start having long talks with De La Hoya. Rivero wanted to train his mind before they got into the boxing ring. He wanted him to start concentrating more on defense. Rivero wanted De La Hoya to realize that a fighter who is not hurt always has a better chance to win.

Working with Rivero gave De La Hoya a lot of his old confidence back. "I can knock anybody out," he said, "if they stay and fight. Even then, I can usually catch up with them."

De La Hoya's first fight with Rivero as his trainer was a championship bout against IBF Lightweight Champion Rafael Ruelas on May 6, 1995. De La Hoya moved up in weight and abandoned his WBO Junior Lightweight belt.

De La Hoya used many of the old trainer's moves, and he scored an amazing second-round knockout of a tough fighter and champion. De La Hoya improved his record to 18–0, and earned his third championship belt. He was now the IBF Lightweight Champion. After the fight, De La Hoya was very excited about his new trainer.

"He's [Rivero] basically taught me that I can box anybody," De La Hoya said. "He's taught me to keep opponents off balance. When I was knocked down early in my career, well, it never would have happened if I'd had the Professor."

De La Hoya also used advice from his thirteen-year-old sister, Ceci, in his strategy. "Don't be dumb, I don't want you to get hit," she told him before the fight. "Just hurry up, make your money and get out of there, so you can spend more time with me."

De La Hoya's family and friends are very important to him. Besides spending time with his sister, he still wanted to keep both Rivero and Alcazar in his corner. The longtime family friend and trainer was rewarded with a five-year contract to keep everybody happy and together.

During this time, De La Hoya trained at Big Bear Lake, California, and spent his spare time reading horror books by Stephen King and listening to music by Mariah Carey. His favorite television show is *America's Funniest Home Videos*. Of course, training and hard work always came first.

De La Hoya's next bout was against another tough opponent. He was going up against the undefeated Gennaro Hernandez. Once again, the fight was in Los Angeles, and once again, fight fans did not support De La Hoya as he expected them to. There were no empty seats this time, but most of the fight fans rooted openly for the Mexican, Hernandez. They even booed De La Hoya!

Hernandez was the current Junior Lightweight Champion, but he had moved up in weight to fight De La Hoya. Hernandez was 34–0, and was a very well-respected fighter.

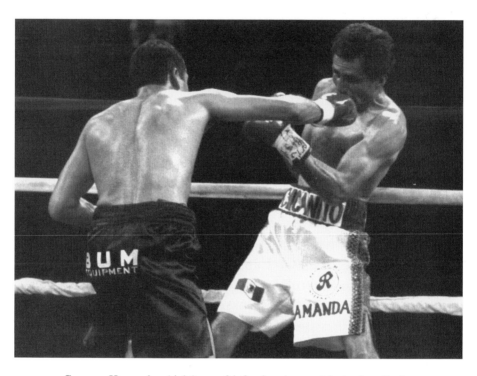

Gennaro Hernandez (right) was 34–0 when he went in to face De La Hoya. After Hernandez came out he had his first loss and a nose that was broken in twenty-two places.

De La Hoya gave him a beating and scored a sixth-round TKO when Hernandez was unable to continue. Hernandez waved off the referee as the seventh round was scheduled to begin, signaling that he could not go on. De La Hoya had broken Hernandez's nose in twenty-two places! De La Hoya was rewarded with his largest purse, or paycheck, for a single fight: $2.4 million.

Even though there was little support for De La Hoya in his hometown, he often visited schools in the poorer areas to speak to the children. He started the Oscar De La Hoya Foundation to help needy kids. The Foundation purchased the Resurrection Boxing Gym, where De La Hoya trained as a young boy. The gym has been renamed the Oscar De La Hoya Youth Boxing Center.

De La Hoya feels it is important to stress education and self-esteem to all young people. "We should all feel equal," he says. "I grew up without having anything in life; I had to struggle, so I can relate to them."

However, De La Hoya was so disappointed in his lack of fan support that he even considered retiring from boxing and going back to school. He was very hurt that his hometown had rejected him as a hero. "I grew up here and now that I am successful they don't like that. The criticism is the worst here. They think I've forgotten about them, but I haven't."

Soon De La Hoya would find acceptance. Surprisingly, it happened three thousand miles from home. He fought in New York City's Madison Square Garden in December 1995, as the headliner in a fight against former champ Jesse James Leija. The promoters at Madison Square Garden were hoping to attract eleven thousand people for the fight. They wound up with sixteen thousand!

The fans chanted De La Hoya's name and cheered his every move. He went hard after Leija in the first round. After

Charging ahead, Oscar De La Hoya backs Jesse James Leija up against the ropes. De La Hoya only needed two rounds to earn the knockout.

the round, a stunned Leija knew the end was near. "He hits hard, man," Leija told his trainer between the first and second rounds. "I didn't know how much power he has."

De La Hoya knocked out Leija in the next round. It was the first time that Leija had ever been counted out of a fight. Even more fascinating was the fact that Leija joined a growing list of ex-champions whom De La Hoya had beaten. In only three and a half years of professional boxing, De La Hoya had already defeated seven current or former champions: Troy Dorsey, Jimmi Bredhal, Jorge Paez, John John Molina, Rafael Ruelas, Gennaro Hernandez, and Leija.

De La Hoya was pleased with the fan support. "The

Trying to land a finishing blow, Oscar De La Hoya (right) looks to put
the hurt on Darryl Tyson.

American fans are always with me," a jubilant De La Hoya said after the fight. "It's going to take winning fights, and time, for the [Hispanic-American] fans to be on my side."

Now, De La Hoya and the promoters had a list of championship fighters that they wanted to face. Winning these bouts would place Oscar De La Hoya as one of the greatest fighters of all time. Some of the names on the list were Julio Cesar Chavez, Pernell "Sweet Pea" Whitaker, Felix Trinidad, Hector "Macho" Camacho, and "Terrible" Terry Norris.

De La Hoya would not duck or hide from any of these great fighters. He wanted to be known as one of the best ever, and he knew the only way would be to face and defeat these fighters.

De La Hoya defeated Darryl Tyson in two rounds that February, in what was really a tune-up fight for his bout against his boyhood idol, Chavez.

The fight against Chavez was arranged and scheduled for the following June. De La Hoya's path to greatness would face its most difficult stretch.

# *Chapter 6*

De La Hoya bloodied his boyhood idol, Julio Cesar Chavez, and won by a TKO. The fight lasted only four rounds. De La Hoya was now WBC Super Lightweight Champion.

The Golden Boy was truly golden, a superstar. He was speeding toward all-time greatness. He was now famous, and rich beyond his dreams. Yet something still drove De La Hoya to keep fighting. He wanted to be the best fighter in the world. "I want to become a legend in boxing," he said.

After his impressive win, there would be other huge paydays on the way. Looming ahead for him was a fight against Pernell "Sweet Pea" Whitaker. Many boxing experts considered Whitaker to be the best boxer, pound for pound, in the sport. It was a fight that fans, reporters, and the fighters wanted.

But first, De La Hoya would have to fight Miguel Angel Gonzalez in a title fight to defend his Super Lightweight title. Gonzalez was the current Junior Lightweight Champion. He gained weight to move up and fight De La Hoya. Although Gonzalez sported an incredible 40–0 record, he was relatively unknown outside Mexico. In fact, he had never even fought outside Mexico.

The fight, which would be on January 18, 1997, was being regarded as a tune-up fight for De La Hoya. De La Hoya may have been thinking ahead to his fight against Whitaker. The only problem was that Gonzalez did not consider himself to be a warm-up.

Gonzalez attacked De La Hoya. He constantly kept coming forward. He threw right hand after big right hand. He did not back up at all, and he had De La Hoya in trouble on several occasions. De La Hoya was unable to bully Gonzalez or hurt him. He had to rely on his superior boxing skills to outpoint the tough Gonzalez. De La Hoya did have Gonzalez in trouble in the fifth, but Gonzalez stayed on his feet and continued fighting.

In the tenth round of a scheduled twelve-round fight, Gonzalez hit De La Hoya with a hard right hand that partially closed his left eye. The eye became red and puffy. It was the first time in De La Hoya's career that he looked as if he had been in a fight.

De La Hoya held on to win a unanimous decision and did not give the tough Gonzalez a lot of credit. "I was prepared physically and whatever he did to me did not catch my attention," De La Hoya told reporters after the fight. "That bruise under my eye was not a big distraction."

Even though he was in great shape physically, De La Hoya was clearly looking ahead to the scheduled fight against Whitaker.

He admitted that all the talk about the fight with Whitaker made it hard to focus on Gonzalez. "Everywhere I'd go, people would be talking about Pernell Whitaker," De La Hoya said. "A lot of people were very positive on me winning this fight easily. But just me thinking about Pernell Whitaker in the future and thinking that I had just beat Chavez . . . but you have this guy in between who is 40–0 that really doesn't present a big threat. Mentally, I really wasn't too focused."

The fight against Whitaker was the next step for De La Hoya on his road to greatness. The winner of the Welterweight Championship fight would be regarded by many as the best fighter, pound for pound, in the world. This would not be an easy fight for De La Hoya. Whitaker is a southpaw, meaning that he fights left-handed. He also has a very quick and awkward style that makes a lot of fighters miss him when they are throwing punches.

De La Hoya and his cornerpeople would have to come up with a good strategy to defeat Whitaker, the Welterweight Champion. "We're going to figure out maybe three or four different game plans for Pernell Whitaker. Whitaker has a very different style, a very awkward style. But we can figure something out; that's what a champion is all about," De La Hoya said before the fight.

The thirty-three-year-old Whitaker, 40–1–1, had a game plan of his own. "I have to take advantage of my experience over him," he said. "This kid is an excellent fighter and I give him credit but, right now, he's just not ready."

The fight took place on April 12, 1997, at the Thomas & Mack Center in Las Vegas. From the first bell it was clear that this fight would not be a typical slugfest. It would be a cat-and-mouse fight—little punches here, a jab there, and both fighters constantly moving and staying just out of each other's reach.

Whitaker, who had won six championships, frustrated De La Hoya with his quickness and his artful style. De La Hoya was unable to land two solid shots in a row for the entire fight. Part of his fight plan was to go southpaw himself. On several occasions, he turned around and fought left-handed. This

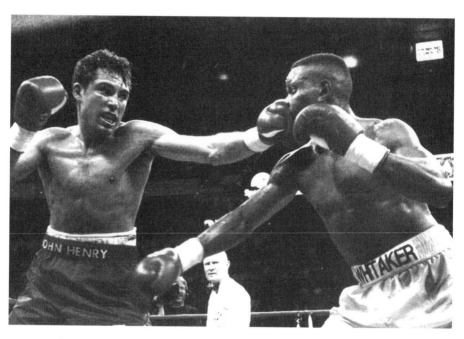

On April 12, 1997, De La Hoya (left) fought Pernell "Sweet Pea" Whitaker for the WBC Welterweight Championship.

seemed to confuse Whitaker, and De La Hoya landed several good right-handed jabs to the head.

Whitaker danced and maneuvered, but he did not throw many punches. He was, however, credited with a knockdown in the ninth round. He punched De La Hoya as the two fighters' feet became entangled, and De La Hoya went down.

It was a tough fight for both fighters, and De La Hoya resorted to an old amateur boxing trick in order to score points. He tried to finish every round with a flurry of punches. He hoped to show the judges that he was the more active fighter. Judges sometimes award an evenly fought round to the more active fighter.

The fight lasted all twelve rounds and was very close. Both fighters waited nervously as the judges tallied their scorecards. One judge scored the fight 9–3, another 9–2–1, and the third judge scored it 8–4 for a seemingly one-sided victory for the new WBC Welterweight Champion of the World, Oscar De La Hoya.

The bout seemed much closer to Whitaker than that, and he was very angry about the outcome. "This doesn't make sense, because I destroyed the kid," a bitter Whitaker said after the fight.

De La Hoya earned $10 million for the fight, and he received his fourth championship title belt. He thought the judges scored the fight correctly, but also felt that he did not look his best against the tough Whitaker. He claimed a lot of it had to do with wrong instructions from his corner. "I was confused, inside the ring I was confused," he said. "The Professor [Rivero] kept telling me to move to my right, that's the perfect game plan. Then, after the fight, everyone said that I did everything wrong. I had to move to my left. Your trainer has to help you."

According to most boxing experts, a fighter should always

try to move to his left when he fights a southpaw. This stops the left-handed fighter from being able to use his left cross, or his left hook. De La Hoya felt that Rivero should have told him this.

Once again De La Hoya decided to change trainers. He let Rivero go and brought in veteran trainer Emanuel Steward. De La Hoya said that letting Rivero go had nothing to do with the Whitaker fight. He simply felt that he needed to regain his good offensive knockout form. "He [Rivero] taught me everything that there is to know about defense," De La Hoya explained. "Everything I did wrong, I blame myself. In my last three fights, I haven't had a clean knockout."

Steward became the fourth trainer in De La Hoya's short but brilliant boxing career. Switching trainers so many times seems to be the only bad mark on an otherwise perfect career. Many boxing experts believe that it benefits a fighter to form a long-term relationship with a trainer. This way the two men think the same way and know what to expect from each other.

In any event, Steward quickly revitalized De La Hoya's lost knockout punch. His next fight, a June 1997 bout against David Kamau, was a short one. Even though Kamau had a nine-inch reach advantage against De La Hoya, it did not help. De La Hoya knocked out the young African fighter in the second round, to run his record to 25–0.

Next up for De La Hoya, was former champ Hector "Macho" Camacho. Camacho is a veteran fighter who had never been knocked out. In the ninth round, De La Hoya floored Camacho after hitting him with four punches. It was only the second time in Camacho's career that he had been knocked down. Although, De La Hoya was not able to knock Camacho out, De La Hoya did win a unanimous decision to keep his welterweight title.

After the Camacho fight, De La Hoya changed trainers

once again. Steward was dismissed and Alcazar would be De La Hoya's trainer for his fight against Wilfredo Rivera. On December 6, 1997, De La Hoya beat Rivera and remained undefeated.

After taking time off because of a wrist injury, De La Hoya returned to the ring in on June 13, 1998. De La Hoya was set to fight Frenchman Patrick Charpentier, in El Paso, Texas. This time the Mexican-American fans welcomed De La Hoya with open arms. He did not disappoint. In front of one of the largest crowds in boxing history, De La Hoya won easily. The referee stopped the fight in the early stages of the third round when Charpentier could not continue.

In the fall of 1997, De La Hoya (left) fought the flashy, and dangerous, Hector Camacho. Known as the "Macho Man," Camacho is regarded as a fighter who is very difficult to knock down.

De La Hoya celebrates retaining his championship belt after a fight with Wilfredo Rivera. A great champion, De La Hoya may be a fighter for the ages.

It seems that whatever he wants to master, offense or defense, he is capable of doing both. Even at a young age, De La Hoya is aware of his growing place in boxing history. He realizes that he can be one of the best ever to fight. Because of that belief, he is committed to his sport. He does not drink or smoke, and he takes his training very seriously. For the two months before fighting Chavez, De La Hoya trained at a log cabin in the woods. He designed the cabin himself. His only entertainment was watching boxing and golf on television.

De La Hoya calls his formula for success, "the three Ds"— dedication, discipline, and desire. "I've never seen a kid like this," Arum said. "His total focus is on boxing."

"I'll dedicate myself to boxing," De La Hoya said. "Then I can do whatever I want later on." His plan is to fight into his late twenties and then retire. He hopes to win six titles. Then he would like to go back to school and become an architect. He even sees a direct link between boxing and architecture. "Boxing is an art form," he says. "You have to be really good at it to know what you are doing. You have to create your game plan in your mind and work at it. When I draw a house plan," he continued, "I think about it, visualize it as I do in boxing . . . and it becomes beautiful. The ring is my canvas."

Oscar De La Hoya's whole life has been dedicated to boxing. The magical ride that he is on started with a Christmas gift when he was three years old. Luckily for boxing fans, it shows no sign of ending soon.

# Career Statistics

| DATE | OPPONENT | OUTCOME | RECORD |
|------|----------|---------|--------|
| Nov. 23, 1992 | Lamar Williams | 1st round knockout | 1–0 |
| Dec. 12, 1992 | Cliff Hicks | 1st round knockout | 2–0 |
| Jan. 3, 1993 | Paris Alexander | 2nd round knockout | 3–0 |
| Feb. 6, 1993 | Curtis Strong | 4th round knockout | 4–0 |
| Mar. 13, 1993 | Jeff Mayweather | 4th round knockout | 5–0 |
| Apr. 6, 1993 | Mike Grable | Won by decision | 6–0 |
| May 8, 1993 | Frankie Avelar | 4th round knockout | 7–0 |
| June 7, 1993 | Troy Dorsey | 1st round knockout | 8–0 |
| Aug. 14, 1993 | Reynaldo Carter | 6th round knockout | 9–0 |
| Aug. 27, 1993 | Angelo Nunez | 4th round knockout | 10–0 |
| Oct. 30, 1993 | Narcisco Valenzuela | 1st round knockout | 11–0 |
| Mar. 5, 1994 | Jimmy Bredhal | 10th round knockout | 12–0 |
| May 27, 1994 | Giorgio Campanella | 3rd round knockout | 13–0 |
| July 29, 1994 | Jorge Paez | 2nd round knockout | 14–0 |
| Nov. 18, 1994 | Carl Griffith | 3rd round knockout | 15–0 |
| Dec. 10, 1994 | John Avila | 9th round knockout | 16–0 |
| Feb. 18, 1995 | John-John Molina | Won by decision | 17–0 |
| May 6, 1995 | Rafael Ruelas | 2nd round knockout | 18–0 |
| Sep. 9, 1995 | Gennaro Hernandez | 6th round knockout | 19–0 |
| Dec. 15, 1995 | Jesse James Leija | 2nd round knockout | 20–0 |
| Feb. 9, 1996 | Darryl Tyson | 2nd round knockout | 21–0 |
| June 7, 1996 | Julio Cesar Chavez | 4th round knockout | 22–0 |
| Jan. 18, 1997 | Miguel Angel Gonzalez | Won by decision | 23–0 |
| Apr. 12, 1997 | Pernell Whitaker | Won by decision | 24–0 |
| June 14, 1997 | David Kamau | 2nd round knockout | 25–0 |
| Sep. 13, 1997 | Hector Camacho | Won by decision | 26–0 |
| Dec. 6, 1997 | Wilfredo Rivera | 8th round knockout | 27–0 |
| June 13, 1998 | Patrick Charpentier | 3rd round knockout | 28–0 |

# *Where to Write Oscar De La Hoya:*

Mr. Oscar De La Hoya
Top Rank
3900 Paradise Road, Suite 227
Las Vegas, NV  89102

*On the Internet at:* http://www.oscardelahoya.com

# *Index*